T0191171

A Note from
Mary Pope Osborne About the

MAGIC TREE HOUSE® FACT TRACKERS

When I write Magic Tree House® adventures, I love including facts about the times and places Jack and Annie visit. But when readers finish these adventures, I want them to learn even more. So that's why we write a series of nonfiction books that are companions to the fiction titles in the Magic Tree House® series. We call these books Fact Trackers because we love to track the facts! Whether we're researching dinosaurs, pyramids, Pilgrims, sea monsters, or cobras, we're always amazed at how wondrous and surprising the real world is. We want you to experience the same wonder we do—so get out your pencils and notebooks and hit the trail with us. You can be a Magic Tree House® Fact Tracker, too!

Mary Pope Osborne

Here's what kids, parents, and teachers have to say about the Magic Tree House® Fact Trackers:

"They are so good. I can't wait for the next one. All I can say for now is prepare to be amazed!" —Alexander N.

"I have read every Magic Tree House book there is. The [Fact Trackers] are a thrilling way to get more information about the special events in the story." —John R.

"These are fascinating nonfiction books that enhance the magical time-traveling adventures of Jack and Annie. I love these books, especially *American Revolution*. I was learning so much, and I didn't even know it!" —Tori Beth S.

"[They] are an excellent 'behind-the-scenes' look at what the [Magic Tree House fiction] has started in your imagination! You can't buy one without the other; they are such a complement to one another." —Erika N., mom

"Magic Tree House [Fact Trackers] took my children on a journey from Frog Creek, Pennsylvania, to so many significant historical events! The detailed manuals are a remarkable addition to the classic fiction Magic Tree House books we adore!" —Jenny S., mom

"[They] are very useful tools in my classroom, as they allow for students to be part of the planning process. Together, we find facts in the [Fact Trackers] to extend the learning introduced in the fictional companions. Researching and planning classroom activities, such as our class Olympics based on facts found in *Ancient Greece and the Olympics*, help create a genuine love for learning!" —Paula H., teacher

MAGIC TREE HOUSE® FACT TRACKER

Abraham Lincoln

A NONFICTION COMPANION TO MAGIC TREE HOUSE MERLIN MISSION #19:

Abe Lincoln at Last!

BY MARY POPE OSBORNE
AND NATALIE POPE BOYCE

ILLUSTRATED BY SAL MURDOCCA

A STEPPING STONE BOOK™

Random House 🏠 New York

Text copyright © 2011 by Mary Pope Osborne and Natalie Pope Boyce
Illustrations copyright © 2011 by Sal Murdocca
Cover photograph courtesy of the Library of Congress

The Magic Tree House Fact Tracker series was formerly known as the Magic Tree House
Research Guide series. Magic Tree House Merlin Mission #19 was formerly known as
Magic Tree House #47.

Visit us on the Web!
SteppingStonesBooks.com
randomhousekids.com
MagicTreeHouse.com

Educators and librarians, for a variety of teaching tools, visit us at
RHTeachersLibrarians.com

Library of Congress Cataloging-in-Publication Data
Osborne, Mary Pope.
Abraham Lincoln / by Mary Pope Osborne and Natalie Pope Boyce ;
illustrated by Sal Murdocca.
 p. cm. — (Magic tree house fact tracker)
"A nonfiction companion to Magic tree house, #47: Abe Lincoln at last!"
"A Stepping stone book."
ISBN 978-0-375-87024-8 (trade) — ISBN 978-0-375-97024-5 (lib. bdg.) —
ISBN 978-0-375-98861-5 (ebook)
1. Lincoln, Abraham, 1809–1865—Juvenile literature. 2. Presidents—United States—
Biography—Juvenile literature. I. Boyce, Natalie Pope. II. Murdocca, Sal, ill. III. Title.
E457.905.O77 2011 973.7092—dc22 [B] 2011013116

Printed in the United States of America
22 21 20

This book has been officially leveled by using the F&P Text Level Gradient™
Leveling System.

For Jeremy Greensmith, Simone Dinnerstein,
and Adrian David Greensmith

Historical Consultant:

JAMES M. CORNELIUS, Ph.D., Curator, Lincoln Collection, Abraham
Lincoln Presidential Library and Museum

Education Consultant:

HEIDI JOHNSON, language acquisition and science education specialist,
Bisbee, Arizona

With special thanks to the great folks at Random House: Gloria Cheng; Mallory
Loehr; Chelsea Eberly, our indispensable photo researcher; Sal Murdocca, who
always creates the best art; and our editor, the inordinately brave and plucky
Diane Landolf

ABRAHAM
LINCOLN

Contents

Dear Readers,

In <u>Abe Lincoln at Last!</u>, we shared great adventures with President Lincoln. We were with him when he was a boy and also when he became president. In fact, we liked being with Lincoln so much that we hated to leave his side. We really wanted to know everything about him and his world. So we got out our notebooks, and with the help of books and the Internet, we began to track the facts about Abraham Lincoln.

We researched what it was like to live in a log cabin. We even learned how to build a log cabin, just like the one President Lincoln grew up in. We read about his short time in school and how he rose from being a poor boy

to become the sixteenth president of the United States! (We also found out that President Lincoln was a great father and let his little boys run wild in the White House!)

The facts filled our notebooks. Every time we'd write down a new one, we'd learn ten more. So if you're curious about Abraham Lincoln's beard, his family, his great work during the Civil War, and his brave spirit, come with us and follow Abraham Lincoln to the White House! We promise that you'll end up loving Abraham Lincoln as much as we do.

Jack
Annie

1

Abraham Lincoln

Abraham Lincoln was born near Hodgenville, Kentucky, on February 12, 1809. His
birthplace was a one-room log cabin at Sinking Spring Farm along Nolin Creek. The
cabin had one window covered with greased
paper, one door hung by leather straps, and
a fire burning in the fireplace. Outside, the
wind blew through chinks in the logs, chill-
ing the room and making the fire sputter.

Abraham and his mother, Nancy, slept

under bearskin blankets on a mattress made of corn husks. Nearby, his two-year-old sister, Sarah, played on the dirt floor by the dim light of the fireplace. Thomas Lincoln, the baby's father, told his wife he felt proud to have a son.

Abraham's Parents

At this time Kentucky was part of Virginia. It became a state in 1792.

Thomas Lincoln had come to Kentucky as a boy with his family in 1782. His father hoped to start a new life with a larger farm than the one they had owned in Virginia.

The trip from Virginia was long, slow, and dangerous. There were few roads. Mostly there were just overgrown paths. Much of the country was wilderness where bobcats, wolves, and bears roamed the fields and forests. A horse-drawn

14

wagon could cover twenty-five miles a day.
Oxcarts traveled only about half of that.

Like many other settlers, the Lincolns followed
    the Cumberland Trail, a rough road that
        stretched from Kentucky to Tennessee.

The Shawnee, Cherokee, and other Native Americans had lived or hunted in Kentucky for thousands of years. Settlers were taking over their land and pushing them out.

By 1790, over 1,500 settlers had been killed in Kentucky.

There was great tension between the groups. Thomas was just eight when he saw his father killed by a Shawnee war party.

Thomas Lincoln was marked forever by the terror of that day. Abraham said that from then on, his father became a "wandering, laboring boy" who did odd jobs, often working as a carpenter.

Thomas never went to school and almost never wrote more than his signature.

In 1806, Tom married a young woman named Nancy Hanks. She, too, had come from Virginia. Nancy was known for her quick mind and gentle ways. A year later, the Lincolns had Sarah. When their son

16

was born two years later, they named him Abraham, after his grandfather.

Nancy's cousin, Dennis Hanks, was only nine when he first visited the new baby. Later he said that Abraham was the smallest, most "cryin'est" baby he had ever seen. Dennis told Nancy that he didn't think Abraham would ever be worth much. He couldn't have known that someday this tiny, weak infant would become one of the greatest presidents in the history of the United States.

Come with us to learn more about the Lincolns' journeys.

CUMBERLAND
← TRAIL →

KENTUCKY
100 MILES

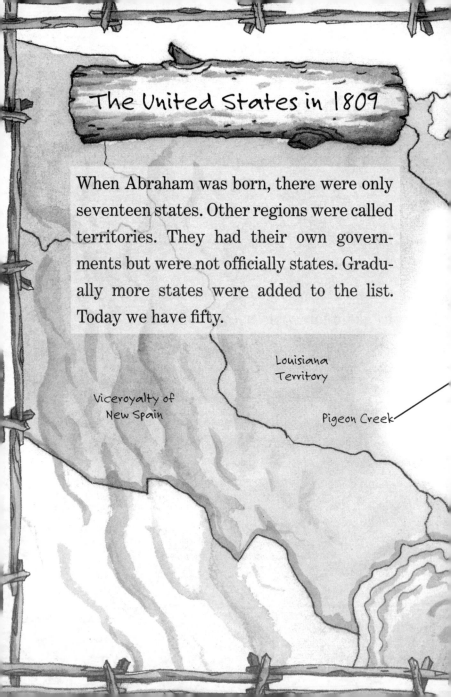

The United States in 1809

When Abraham was born, there were only seventeen states. Other regions were called territories. They had their own governments but were not officially states. Gradually more states were added to the list. Today we have fifty.

Louisiana Territory

Viceroyalty of New Spain

Pigeon Creek

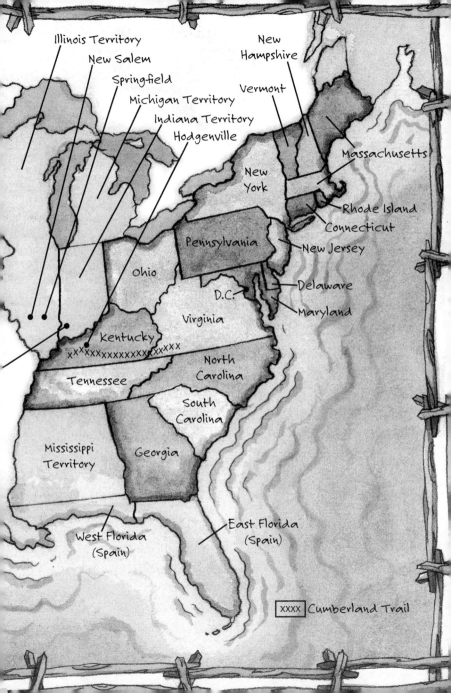

Illinois Territory

New Salem

Springfield

Michigan Territory

Indiana Territory

Hodgenville

New Hampshire

Vermont

Massachusetts

New York

Rhode Island

Connecticut

New Jersey

Pennsylvania

Delaware

D.C.

Maryland

Ohio

Virginia

Kentucky

xxxxxxxxxxxxxxxxxxxx

Tennessee

North Carolina

South Carolina

Mississippi Territory

Georgia

West Florida (Spain)

East Florida (Spain)

xxxx Cumberland Trail

2

The Early Years

When Abraham was two, his parents moved about ten miles away to Knob Creek. Thomas worked hard, but times were tough. When his family needed meat, he grabbed his musket and headed for the nearby woods. The Lincolns survived on deer, wild turkeys, geese, squirrels, and rabbits. Abraham said later that his family lived in "pretty pinching times." Like many others, the Lincolns were very poor.

Life on Knob Creek

When he was old enough, Abraham often helped his father. One Saturday, he spent the day planting pumpkins while his father planted corn. Over and over again, the boy pressed pumpkin seeds into tiny mounds of dirt. That night, a heavy rain washed away the field, seeds and all.

After another downpour, Knob Creek overflowed its banks. One day, Abraham and his friend Austin Gollaher decided to wade across the swollen creek. Suddenly Abraham fell and was swept away by the swirling water! Austin thought fast. He grabbed a long sycamore stick and dragged his sinking friend to safety.

Buckskins and a Raccoon Cap

Nancy Lincoln and little Sarah worked long hours cooking, washing, sewing, spinning, and weaving. In those days, there were no machines to help them.

All the cooking was done in heavy iron pots over an open fire in the fireplace.

Nancy dressed her son in a raccoon cap and a buckskin shirt and pants. Abraham went barefoot most of the year. When the weather got too cold, he wore leather moccasins.

He was a tall, skinny, big-eared boy who grew quickly. His pants were usually several inches above his ankles.

Blab Schools

Abraham's mother told him Bible stories, but it's not certain whether she could read or write. There were no books or paper in the house. In those days, there were very few schools. Being unable to read was not at all unusual.

Thomas Lincoln didn't believe in education. Sometimes he did let his children go to school for a short while. Sarah held her little brother's hand as they trudged two miles to a log cabin school with a dirt floor. Children of all ages sat on rough benches. They wrote on slate boards with chalk.

Their school was called a blab school because the students said their lessons out loud. The teacher had a book or two, but these were the only books in the classroom!

Blab comes from blabber, which means to talk a lot and not make much sense.

25

Early school

Teachers needed no training. Almost anyone who could read well could teach. Many teachers were older teenagers.

After the teacher taught a lesson, the children repeated it back. The classroom was very, very noisy.

In spite of this, Abraham learned to read. The rest of his life he enjoyed

26

reading books, poetry, and plays aloud to others.

When planting and harvest times rolled around, the classroom emptied out. The children were in the fields working. Abraham spent very little time at his first school.

Storytelling

The Lincolns' cabin was within sight of the Cumberland Trail. Even though life on Knob Creek was often lonely, visitors sometimes stopped to chat.

Peddlers selling pots and pans, settlers in wagons, and travelers of all kinds often passed by. The Lincolns also saw black slaves and the white slave traders who were taking them to cities to be sold.

Everyone liked to listen to Tom Lincoln.

He was a born storyteller. Abraham sat nearby, quietly taking in every word his father said.

Afterward he'd practice telling the stories to himself. Then he'd try them out on his friends. Like his father, Abraham became a skilled storyteller and mimic. People loved to listen to him as he spun his tales. This skill came in very handy when he grew up and made speeches.

Off to Indiana

When Abraham was seven, Thomas decided to make a fresh start somewhere else. Problems had arisen about the ownership of his property. Thomas left to scout out land in the new state of Indiana. It was fall, and the winds were beginning to whip. A bad winter was coming. When Tom got back, the family packed up. They were moving to a settlement in Indiana called Pigeon Creek.

Life in a Log Cabin

Shovel for spreading ashes

Handmade bed with corn-husk mattress

Chest for family's few clothes

Packed-dirt floor

Twig broom

Rifle for hunting and defense

Dishwashing pan

Cast-iron pot

Water bucket

3

Abraham Grows Up

In December 1816, the Lincolns traveled sixty miles to the Ohio River. There they loaded their things onto a flatboat and crossed over into Indiana. When they got to the other side, they hacked sixteen miles through dense woods to reach their new land. Tom had piled up brush to mark the spot.

Tom and Abraham built a three-sided shelter. Rain and snow swept into the open front, which was covered only by animal skins. Tom kept a fire burning night and day. The family settled down to wait for spring.

Bears, raccoons, deer, and other wild animals roamed the woods around the camp. The family heard panthers screaming in the night. Abraham and Sarah had to walk a mile to get water from a creek.

The Sparrows Arrive

When the weather got warmer, Tom began building a cabin. First he cut down trees to make logs. Instead of using nails, he notched the logs so that they fit together. Then he stuffed mud or wood chips in the spaces between the logs and cut out a door and window. Finally Thomas built a stone fireplace and packed down dirt and gravel for the floor. When he finished, he began to clear the land for crops.

That fall, Nancy's cousins, Thomas and Betsy Sparrow, arrived with Dennis Hanks, who was now a teenager. The Sparrows had been like parents to Nancy, and she was glad to see them. The Sparrows and Dennis moved into the old shelter. Together the family cleared six acres for planting the next spring.

Milk Sickness

Spring and summer passed without problems. In the fall, a disease called milk sickness struck the family. Back then, people knew that milk caused the illness, but no one knew why. Today we know that if cows eat a plant called white snakeroot, a poison gets into the milk.

White snakeroot

35

In the 1800s, thousands died from this illness, often in Kentucky and Indiana, where the plant grew everywhere. Milk sickness caused trembling, vomiting, stomach pains, and usually death. There was no cure.

People often died of disease in the 1800s. There were few trained doctors, poor medicine, and little knowledge of what cured illnesses.

First the Sparrows got sick and died. Then two weeks later, Nancy got sick. The nearest doctor was thirty-five miles away. But even if he had been closer, he could not have helped.

Before she died, Nancy asked Abraham and Sarah to help their father and to be good and kind. Abraham was only nine years old. He loved his mother with his whole heart. Later he would say that all he ever was in life, he owed to her. Tom, Abraham, and Dennis built a coffin and buried Nancy on a hill next to where the Sparrows lay.

Alone in the Woods

After Nancy died, the family was desperate. Candles and soap began to run out. Clothes became ragged and dirty. Sarah

Soap and candles were made by hand. There were no stores near the cabin.

37

did what she could, but she was only a child. Abraham and Sarah needed a mother.

Tom headed back to Kentucky to find another wife. Now Dennis and the Lincoln children were alone. The winter wind whistled around the cabin, which had nothing more than a bearskin to cover the door. Attracted by pigs that the family kept, panthers prowled around the farm at night. Inside the cabin, Dennis, Sarah, and Abraham huddled together under their ragged blankets.

A New Mother

When Tom returned, he brought a new wife named Sarah, who had her three children with her. Sarah was a widow whom Tom had known for much of his life. Sarah later said that when she arrived, Dennis, Sarah,

and Abraham were so tattered, thin, and
dirty that they didn't look quite human.

Whitewash was like a cheap form of paint. It was often used on cabin walls.

After cleaning everyone up, Sarah Lincoln set about scrubbing the grimy cabin and *whitewashing* the walls. Then she made Tom put in a wooden floor and a strong wooden door hung by leather hinges.

Sarah was a kind woman who treated her stepchildren as her own. She once said Abraham was the best boy she ever knew. He was devoted to her all his life.

Abraham and Books

Abraham went to school when he could. He walked four and a half miles each way to get there. It would take about an hour each way.

That's nine miles a day!

He became the best speller in the class. Sometimes he wrote with a goose or turkey quill that he filled with ink

40

This famous painting shows Abraham sitting by the fire with a book.

made from berries. Other times, he wrote in the dust with a stick, on boards with charcoal, and on shovels with soapstone. He copied math problems onto a wooden board, shaved them off with a knife, and started again.

Abraham said he got his education "by littles." In all, he never had more than about a year of school. Imagine if you stopped after first grade!

Books

Abraham loved to read. His biggest problem was finding books. Most of the people he knew didn't own any. There were no libraries or bookstores. He constantly searched the countryside for anyone who could lend him a book.

If he was lucky enough to find a book, Abraham carried it under his arm everywhere he went. When he finished his chores, he read; when he had any free time, he read. At night, by the dim light of a candle or the fire, he'd read until dawn.

If Abraham couldn't understand something, he read it over and over again. "All I wanted to know was in books," he said. They opened doors to a bigger world and gave him wisdom and strength. He would need both of these all of his life.

Thomas often got angry when he caught Abraham reading while taking a break from his chores.

Once rain ruined a book Abraham had borrowed. He worked for the owner for three days to pay him back.

Abraham Grows Up

At seventeen, Abraham was six feet four inches tall. He was thin but very strong. People claimed he could drive an ax deeper into a log than anyone. Dennis said that hearing Abraham cut trees was like listening to three men working at once.

At Fourth of July picnics, Abraham won wrestling contests with ease. He could lift heavy barrels and once picked up an entire chicken coop!

Leaving Home

Abraham often chopped wood and built fences for people. When he was nineteen, he and two friends took farm produce

Around this time, Abraham's sister, Sarah, died in childbirth.

44

and animals down the Mississippi River to New Orleans on a flatboat. When the job was over, Abraham gave his father all the money he'd earned for three months of work.

When he was twenty-two, he made the trip again. On his second trip, Abraham saw a slave market, where black people were chained, whipped, and treated like animals. He was so shocked he couldn't speak. The sight haunted him for the rest of his life.

There were about two million slaves in America at this time. Most worked on large farms in the South.

Soon after Abraham's second flatboat trip, the family moved to Illinois. His parents stayed there for the rest of their lives.

Abraham was now twenty-two. It was time to make his own way in the world. He headed for the town of New Salem, Illinois.

Abraham the Inventor

When Abraham and his friends were heading for New Orleans on one of their trips, their flatboat got hung up on a dam. Water poured over the boat. Abraham rolled up his pants, jumped out, and cut a hole in the bottom of the boat. Then the men unloaded the flatboat. Since it was lighter, it tilted up and the water on the deck ran out through

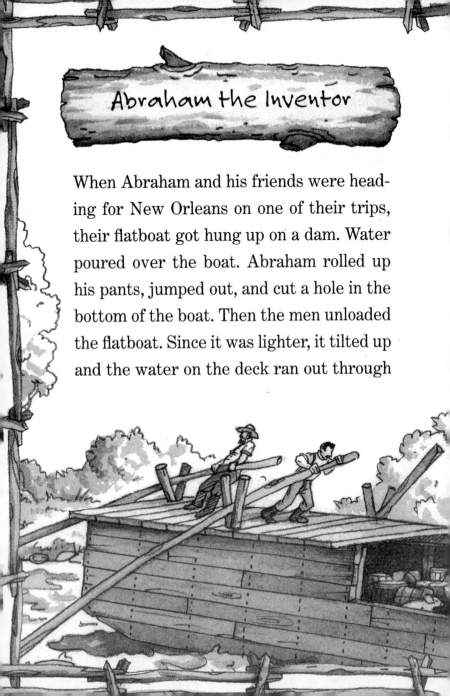

the hole that Abraham had cut. Soon the boat was light enough to float over the dam.

When he was forty, Abraham thought of an invention that would make boats lighter whenever they got stuck. He carved a model boat that showed how this would work.

Abraham got a *patent* for his invention from the United States Patent Office. A patent means that when someone invents something, the invention is theirs alone for a period of time. No one else can make or sell it. Abraham Lincoln is the only president ever to have a patent.

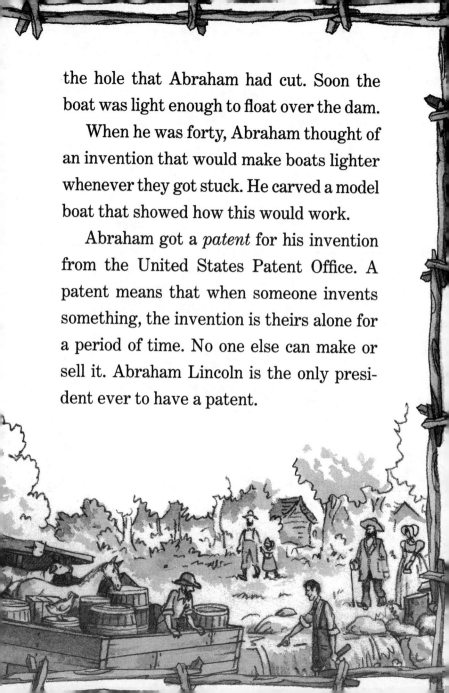

4

The New Salem Years

About twenty-five families lived in New Salem. It had a blacksmith shop, a general store, and other small businesses. There was also a tavern where men gathered to drink and visit with one another. For fun, people got together for dances and for special events such as cabin raisings, quilting bees, footraces, wrestling matches, and horse races.

Abraham found work in a store and lived

in a room in the back. The young man soon became popular with the towns-people. They often stayed at the counter talking and laughing with him. In addition to his stories and jokes, the newcomer also became known for his honesty and hard work. Once Abraham walked six miles to return money to a woman he'd overcharged by accident.

People nicknamed him Honest Abe. But he didn't like to be called Abe, and his friends and family always called him Abraham.

Debating Club

Like a lot of towns at this time, New Salem had a debating club. To debate means to pick a subject and argue opposite sides of it. For example, people might have debated ideas about government, taxes, how to fix the roads, whether paper money was better than gold coins, or whether the death penalty was right or wrong. All of this appealed to Abraham, and he joined the club.

People enjoyed watching the debates. After the speakers finished, judges chose a winner. When Abraham got up to debate, his friends were amazed. They'd expected some funny stories. Instead, they saw a skillful and serious debater. He won many victories.

Abraham and the Clary's Grove Boys

In Abraham's day, people often settled arguments with fistfights or wrestling matches. The Clary's Grove Boys were young men who were wild. They lived in an area near New Salem called Clary's Grove. The boys often roared into town to drink and fight. Everybody stayed out of their way.

One day, a friend bet that Abraham

could win a wrestling match with Jack Armstrong, the strongest man in Clary's Grove. He was said to be as "tough as leather, wiry as a wildcat, and unable to be defeated." The Clary's Grove Boys backed Jack Armstrong.

Abraham didn't like to fight, but he decided he would fight Jack Armstrong. A big crowd gathered. When it looked as if Jack was losing, the Clary's Grove Boys started a big fight. Abraham laughed and jumped right into the middle of it. From then on, the Clary's Grove Boys thought of Abraham as one of their own.

Helpful Friends

Abraham didn't give up his studies. Once he heard that a farmer named John Vance had a grammar book. He walked six miles to John's house to borrow it. Then he asked another clerk in the store to quiz him on it. He studied math books this way as well.

Abraham was friends with a teacher named Mentor Graham. Mentor helped Abraham with grammar and spelling, and they read poems together.

Some of his other friends lent him books

of Shakespeare and other great poets and writers. He often sat with them, talking about what he'd read.

In Abraham's day, people could teach themselves law without going to law school.

One day, Abraham met a young lawyer named John Todd Stuart from nearby Springfield. John urged him to become a lawyer. Abraham liked the idea. Whenever he wasn't working, he'd take law books that he'd borrowed from John, stretch out in a grassy spot, and study for hours.

A Busy Life

The <u>militia</u> was an emergency army of volunteers.

During his six years in New Salem, Abraham worked as a storekeeper, a postmaster, and a land surveyor. Although he never fought, he also served for a short time in the *militia* during the Black Hawk War.

When Abraham delivered mail,
he'd store it in his hat.

Abraham was becoming interested in serving in the government. States all had their own governments, with representatives and senators who made laws.

The federal government in Washington, D.C., also had representatives and senators. They made laws for the whole country.

The general assembly governed the state of Illinois.

In 1834, Abraham won election to the Illinois General Assembly. He borrowed money for a new suit, hopped on a stagecoach, and set out for the state capital, Vandalia.

While he was in Vandalia, Abraham met Stephen Douglas. In the future, Douglas would become his biggest rival. The two men disagreed about slavery. Douglas believed that new states should decide for themselves whether people could own slaves there. Abraham strongly believed that people in the new states should not have the right to own slaves. When he finished his term, Abraham returned to New Salem.

Abraham and Ann

Ann Rutledge was the most popular girl in New Salem. She had a quick mind and a pretty, smiling face. Some said she was

Ann's father owned the Rutledge Tavern, where Abraham sometimes rented a room.

brilliant. Ann even had plans to go to college, which was rare for a woman then. Ann and Abraham became close friends. Even though Ann was engaged to another man, some people thought that she might someday marry Abraham instead.

In the summer of 1835, Ann was twenty-two. A terrible fever hit New Salem. Some of Abraham's close friends died of it. And then Ann Rutledge died. Her death was a blow to Abraham. He later told a friend that the thought of rain or snow falling on Ann's grave made him sad beyond belief.

Almost two years later, in 1837, Abraham left New Salem for Springfield, Illinois, about twenty miles away. Now he wanted to try his hand at being a lawyer. But he never forgot the important years he spent in New Salem.

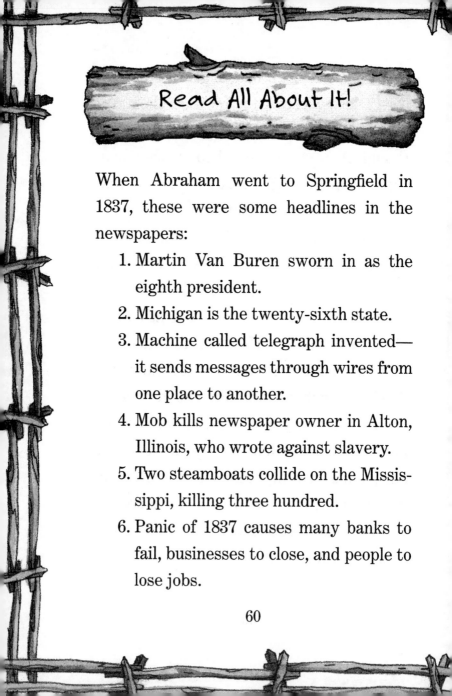

Read All About It!

When Abraham went to Springfield in 1837, these were some headlines in the newspapers:

1. Martin Van Buren sworn in as the eighth president.
2. Michigan is the twenty-sixth state.
3. Machine called telegraph invented—it sends messages through wires from one place to another.
4. Mob kills newspaper owner in Alton, Illinois, who wrote against slavery.
5. Two steamboats collide on the Mississippi, killing three hundred.
6. Panic of 1837 causes many banks to fail, businesses to close, and people to lose jobs.

7. Seminole Indians attack Fort Foster in Florida.

5

The Springfield Years

Abraham rode to Springfield on a borrowed horse. The town had only about 1,300 people. Shops lined the streets around the town square. A brick courthouse stood in the middle of it. Although there were a few beautiful houses, most were simple wooden ones.

The unpaved streets were muddy in the winter and dusty in the summer. Farm animals such as pigs, chickens, and cows

Springfield, 1869

Springfield grew when it became the state capital in 1839.

roamed around at will. Springfield was just a sleepy little town. But after New Salem, it seemed like a big city to Abraham.

Abraham had almost no money and needed a place to stay. On his first day there, he walked into a store and began talking to its owner, Joshua Speed.

Joshua said that Abraham had the saddest face he'd ever seen. Because he felt sorry for him, Joshua offered to share a room with Abraham over the store. He told Abraham he could pay for it later, after he set up his law practice.

Joshua Speed was a well-educated young man from a rich family.

Abraham raced upstairs, threw his saddlebags on the bed, and raced back down. He had a huge smile on his face. "Well, Speed, I am moved!" he said. He lived over the store for four years. Joshua became the closest friend he ever had.

Settling In

Abraham practiced law with his friend John Todd Stuart. Springfield was a welcoming town. There were several schools, a bookstore, and a drama club. The back room at Joshua's store was a popular meeting place. At night, Abraham and his friends sat by the fireplace to laugh, swap stories, talk about books, and discuss different ideas.

While serving in the state legislature in Vandalia, Abraham helped get the capital of Illinois moved to Springfield. (It was moved two years after he arrived.) People were grateful to him. There were invitations to parties, dinners, and dances.

Abraham and Mary Todd

Abraham met Mary Todd at a dance. She was visiting her sisters in Springfield. Mary was well educated, lively, and pretty. She'd studied French, dancing, music, and literature. Her family was one of the most important in Kentucky. They wanted Mary to marry someone wealthy like them.

Abraham Lincoln

Mary Todd Lincoln

Abraham walked shyly up to Mary. "Miss Todd," he said, "I want to dance with you in the worst way." Afterward Mary laughed and said he *did* dance in the worst way!

Mary and Abraham had much in common. They both loved books and had interesting talks about them. They loved politics and were both against slavery. They also had many differences. Mary was outgoing with a quick temper. Abraham was calm and a little shy. Even though Mary's family didn't approve, she married Abraham Lincoln in 1842. Later they bought a house near his office and settled down to raise a family.

Today the Lincoln Home is open to visitors.

The couple had four sons, named Robert, Edward, William, and Thomas. They always called Thomas "Tad" because he wiggled around like a little tadpole, and William became "Willie."

When Abraham got home from the office, the boys would jump on him and wrestle on the floor. Mary said he was the most loving father anyone could have. Sadly, Eddie died of a fever when he was only three. For months, his parents mourned the little boy's death.

Riding the Circuit

Abraham found a new law partner named William Herndon. The two worked together for seventeen years. In those days, judges and lawyers traveled a certain route called a *circuit* (SIR-kit) to hear cases.

Beginning in 1837, when he first became a lawyer, Abraham rode the circuit. For ten years, he followed Judge Samuel Treat. For the next twelve years, Abraham followed Judge David Davis to courtrooms around central Illinois. Riding the circuit was a way of life in the spring and fall. He was

away from home for about ten weeks at a time.

The entire circuit around central Illinois was about a four-hundred-mile journey.

Abraham loved the prairies, with their rolling grasslands. He loved meeting people and trading stories with the other lawyers and townsfolk. Sometimes he even met clients under trees or in taverns. Abraham was a skillful lawyer. And his stories often had the whole courtroom laughing.

Abraham Goes to Washington

In 1846, Abraham ran for the U.S. House of Representatives.

The U.S. House of Representatives and the U.S. Senate make laws for the whole country.

He won the election, and the whole family moved to Washington, D.C. The city was so crowded that the Lincolns all lived together in one room in a boardinghouse. After a few months, Mary and the

Washington, D.C., 1843

boys left for her father's house in Kentucky.

Soon Abraham was caught up in the business of Congress. He made speeches against plans to take over land from Mexico and helped other candidates get elected.

But Abraham missed his family badly. He wrote Mary that nights were lonely. "I hate to stay in this old room by myself," he said. When his term was over, he returned to his law practice in Springfield.

Lincoln–Douglas Debates

Abraham ran for election again in 1858. This time it was for the U.S. Senate. His rival was Stephen Douglas. Stephen Douglas was only five feet four inches tall. In spite of this, people called him the Little Giant because of his large head, broad shoulders, and booming voice.

Stephen Douglas

Abraham and Stephen Douglas still disagreed about slavery. Stephen Douglas was firm that new

73

states and territories should decide for themselves whether to allow slavery. Abraham's opinion was that states with slaves could keep them. But he felt strongly that new states and territories should be free. Abraham and Stephen Douglas decided to hold public debates to argue their different views. The debates took place in seven different towns.

Stephen Douglas was a powerful debater, but so was Abraham. Through the

debates people got to know Abraham and what he stood for. Stephen Douglas was better known, however, and he won the close election.

Two years later, Abraham again faced his old rival. In 1860, the Republican Party chose Abraham Lincoln as their candidate to be the sixteenth president of the United States. He ran against Stephen Douglas again and two other men. This time, Abraham won.

Abraham's Beard

Right before the election, a young girl wrote to Abraham and suggested that he grow a beard. No other president had ever had one.

Grace Bedell was eleven years old. In her letter she said that because his face was so thin, she thought he might look better with "whiskers." She was sure he'd get more votes if he grew a beard. Then Grace asked that he answer her right away.

Abraham wrote her right back. In the letter he said he was worried that people would think he was conceited if he grew one. But he took Grace's idea to heart. President Abraham Lincoln arrived in Washington, D.C., with a new beard.

6

President Abraham Lincoln

On a cold February day, President Lincoln got ready to catch a special train for Washington, D.C. His oldest son, Robert, was with him. Mary and the younger boys were to follow later. The president packed his own trunks. On them he wrote: "A. Lincoln, White House, Washington, D.C."

Over a thousand people waited at the

train station to say good-bye. The president's eyes filled with tears as he shook their hands. He told them how much he loved the town and how much they meant to him. Then he boarded the train. He would never see Springfield again.

Along the way, people lined the tracks to wave and wish the new president well. As the train sped through the night, President Lincoln sat in his private car deep in thought. He knew the United States was facing a very dark time.

The White House

The Lincolns found that life in the White House was hectic. They had their own rooms, but much of the building was open to the public or used for offices. The halls were jammed with people there to ask the president for government jobs. When the doors opened in the morning, hundreds pushed in to get a good place in line.

In those days, people could easily walk in and out of the White House.

President Lincoln saw as many of them as he could. "They don't want much," he said. "They get but little, and I must see them." After an early breakfast, he took a walk around the White House grounds. Then he went down the hall to his office.

President Lincoln's office had a fireplace and two tall windows that looked out over the south lawn. From his chair, he could also see the Washington Monument, which was only half finished, and the Potomac River. He worked there from early morning to late at night.

The Boys Run Wild

The Lincolns were easygoing parents. Tad was almost eight and Willie was ten. The boys kept the White House in an uproar. They raced through the halls and up and down the stairs. They even built a fort on the White House roof.

When they were bored, Willie and Tad rang the servants' bells, and once they ate up all the strawberries that the cooks were saving for a fancy dinner!

The boys loved being with their father. They often burst into cabinet meetings to tell him "important" things. Tad always knocked on the office door with his special signal, three short knocks and two

Willie

Tad

 Abraham Lincoln loved animals and children. They all had the run of the White House.

long ones. One time a visitor came into the office and found President Lincoln pinned to the floor with his two little boys on top of him.

It wasn't unusual for President Lincoln to hold meetings with a boy or a dog on his lap. Tad often fell asleep on the floor beside his father's chair as the president worked late into the night.

North vs. South

President Lincoln faced a terrible problem. Tension had been building between Northern and Southern states for a long time. The two sections of the country were very different. The North had more cities and factories than the South. It also had more skilled workers and more wealth.

Most people in the South were farmers

who grew rice, tobacco, sugarcane, and cotton. Many were small farmers who worked the land themselves. But others owned huge farms called *plantations*. Plantation owners depended on slave labor.

This North Carolina plantation house was built in 1725.

Southerners feared that their voices weren't heard in Washington. They felt that the government was too powerful and taxed them unfairly. They also believed states should make most of their own laws and that slavery was necessary to their survival. Things became so bad that Southern states began to vote to *secede from,* or leave, the United States and become a separate nation.

Most of the slaves lived and worked on farms and plantations in the South.

The Civil War Begins

South Carolina was the first state to secede. Within six weeks, Mississippi, Florida, Alabama, Georgia, Louisiana, and Texas seceded as well. They named their new nation the Confederate States of America and elected Jefferson Davis president. Then, in the three months

Northern states were called the Union. Southern states were called the Confederacy.

Jefferson Davis was sworn in as the first president of the Confederate States of America in Montgomery, Alabama, in 1861.

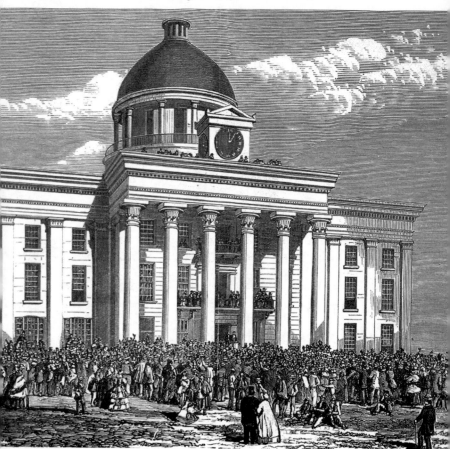

after Lincoln took office, Virginia, Arkansas, North Carolina, and Tennessee joined the Confederacy.

On April 12, 1861, the first shot of the Civil War was heard at Fort Sumter, South Carolina, when Southern soldiers fired cannons at Northern troops on duty there. The Civil War had begun.

In the South, the Civil War was called the War Between the States. Northerners usually called it the Rebellion.

President Lincoln felt he had no choice but to keep the country united and raised an army of about 75,000 volunteers. He thought the war would last about three months.

Instead the Civil War lasted four terrible years. President Lincoln would need many more soldiers. It was the most brutal war in America's history. Over 600,000 men lost their lives. At times battlefields were so littered with bodies, you could hardly see the ground.

Death of Willie

In the midst of the war, in February 1862, Tad and Willie came down with typhoid fever. At first, it looked as if both boys were getting better. But then Willie got worse and died. It was a terrible blow. Like his father, Willie had loved books and learning. He'd been a kind and gentle boy, adored by everyone.

Tad cried for a month, and Mary didn't leave her room for three months. She was never the same. President Lincoln continued to work despite his awful grief. Because his brother Robert was away, Tad was the only son left in the White House.

Robert had left law school to join the Union Army.

The Telegraph Office

The War Department was across the lawn from the White House. People often saw the president's tall figure walking to the War Department's telegraph office. If the weather was cool, he wore a gray plaid shawl draped over his shoulders.

The telegraph helped Lincoln contact his generals every night.

When he got to the office, President Lincoln read reports from his generals about the war. He was always aware of the battles and the numbers killed. Often he would spend the whole night there.

The president looked much older. His face had become lined and sad. Each battle report was hard for him to bear. The loss of lives on both sides seemed almost unbelievable.

Emancipation Proclamation

In September 1862, the president warned the Confederate states that if they didn't rejoin the Union within one hundred days, he would set their slaves free. They refused. So on New Year's Day of 1863, President Lincoln issued an order called the *Emancipation Proclamation.*

It said that slaves in all the states

To emancipate means to set free. A proclamation is a command or order.

92

that were still rebelling against the Union were now "forever free." As word spread throughout the South, slaves cheered their new freedom.

Gettysburg Address

In July 1863, the bloodiest battle in the Civil War took place in Gettysburg, Pennsylvania. More than 172,000 men fought for three days. When it was over, 8,000 men lay dead. The toll of dead and wounded was higher than in any other battle. The North had won, and the tide was beginning to turn.

On November 19, 1863, 15,000 people gathered at the battlefield to honor the soldiers who had died. President Lincoln was there to give a speech. The speaker before him talked for over two hours.

President Lincoln's speech lasted only two minutes. He called for the nation to

The speech was just ten sentences long.

come together again. His speech is known as the *Gettysburg Address*. It is one of the most famous speeches in American history.

The Gettysburg Address said our ancestors believed in a nation where all

Gettysburg Address

people were created equal. It also said that the deaths at Gettysburg were part of an unfinished struggle to give America "a new birth of freedom—and that government of the people, by the people, for the people, shall not perish from the earth."

General Ulysses S. Grant

In 1864, the president chose General Ulysses S. Grant to lead the Union Army. General Grant came from a poor family but had been able to go to West Point. Grant was an excellent general. Robert E. Lee surrendered to him on April 9, 1865. Ulysses S. Grant later served two terms as president of the United States.

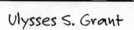
Ulysses S. Grant

96

General Robert E. Lee

Robert E. Lee led the Confederate army during most of the Civil War. He had also graduated from West Point and was from a wealthy, slave-owning family. Lee was also a good general, but he didn't have enough weapons or soldiers. His soldiers loved him. For many years after the war, he remained a hero in the South.

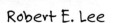

Robert E. Lee

7

The Final Chapter

On November 8, 1864, President Lincoln was elected for a second term. The war was almost over. Five months later, General Lee surrendered to General Grant in Appomattox, Virginia. The South lay in ruins. Most of the battles had been fought on its soil. But both sides had paid a terrible price.

President Lincoln invited the Confederates back into the Union. He asked that they not be crippled by harsh punishment. He began plans to make the country whole again.

Two weeks before he went to Ford's Theatre, President Lincoln dreamed that he would be assassinated.

Ford's Theatre

On Friday, April 14, 1865, President and Mrs. Lincoln went to a play at Ford's Theatre in Washington, D.C. When they arrived, they went upstairs to the president's special box.

The play was funny, and the audience was laughing. Then the door to the president's box softly opened, and a man crept in. He carefully aimed a gun at the back of the president's head and fired. President Lincoln slumped forward, and Mary began screaming.

The man was an actor named John Wilkes Booth. He was a Southerner who hated President Lincoln. Booth leapt over the balcony. He caught his spur on a flag and fell to the stage. Even with a broken leg, he managed to escape on a horse waiting by the back door.

John Wilkes Booth was later caught and killed.

Soldiers carried the president's limp

body to a house across the street. Doctors arrived but saw there was no hope. The bullet had gone into his brain.

People stood by the bed of the unconscious man and listened to his slow, labored breathing. The president's face was calm and peaceful. He died at 7:22 the next morning.

The nation was stunned. Crowds stood in silence as church bells tolled, and stores were draped in black. President Lincoln's hearse rolled through the capital to the train station for the long journey back to Springfield. Willie's coffin was removed from the Washington cemetery and placed on the train near the president's coffin.

It's thought that over 10 million people watched as the funeral train passed through their towns.

The trip was 1,700 miles long. The train traveled through 180 cities and 7 states. At every stop, people stood by to

Lincoln's hearse proceeds through the streets of Washington.

honor the man who'd guided the country through such bitter times.

When the train arrived, Springfield was absolutely still. Flags flew at half-mast.

103

Everyone wore black. Churches filled with people who came to pray and mourn. During the day, the church bells' slow ringing was the only sound that broke the terrible silence. As the president's hearse rumbled through the streets to the cemetery, a family friend led his favorite horse, Old Bob, behind it.

All of Springfield lined the streets. At the cemetery, President Lincoln's friends comforted Robert as the country said a last farewell to one of its finest men.

Today we still remember Abraham Lincoln as an incredible leader. His wisdom helped to free the slaves and save the United States. Every February we celebrate his birthday with a special holiday called Presidents' Day. Abraham Lincoln told great stories, but his own story is one of the greatest of them all.

Doing More Research

There's a lot more you can learn about Abraham Lincoln. The fun of research is seeing how many different sources you can explore.

Books

Most libraries and bookstores have books about Abraham Lincoln.

Here are some things to remember when you're using books for research:

1. You don't have to read the whole book. Check the table of contents and the index to find the topics you're interested in.

2. Write down the name of the book.

When you take notes, make sure you write down the name of the book in your notebook so you can find it again.

3. Never copy exactly from a book.

When you learn something new from a book, put it in your own words.

4. Make sure the book is nonfiction.

Some books tell make-believe stories about Abraham Lincoln. Make-believe stories are called *fiction*. They're fun to read, but not good for research.

Research books have facts and tell true stories. They are called *nonfiction*. A librarian or teacher can help you make sure the books you use for research are nonfiction.

Here are some good nonfiction books about Abraham Lincoln:

- *Abe Lincoln Goes to Washington* by Cheryl Harness

- *Abe's Honest Words: The Life of Abraham Lincoln* by Doreen Rappaport

- *Abraham Lincoln: A Great President, a Great American*, Easy Reader Biographies series, by Violet Findley

- *Lincoln and His Boys* by Rosemary Wells

- *Meet Abraham Lincoln* by Barbara Cary

- *Who Was Abraham Lincoln?* by Janet B. Pascal

- *Young Abe Lincoln* by Cheryl Harness

Museums and Landmarks

Many museums and historic landmarks have exhibits about Abraham Lincoln. These places can help you learn more about him.

When you go to a museum or historic landmark:

1. Be sure to take your notebook!
Write down anything that catches your interest. Draw pictures, too!

2. Ask questions.
There are almost always people at museums and historic landmarks who can help you find what you're looking for.

3. Check the calendar.
Many museums and historic landmarks have special events and activities just for kids!

Here are some museums and historic landmarks that have exhibits about Abraham Lincoln:

- Abraham Lincoln Presidential Library and Museum (Springfield, Illinois)

- Ford's Theatre National Historic Site (Washington, D.C.)

- Gettysburg National Military Park Museum (Pennsylvania)

- Lincoln Heritage Museum (Lincoln, Illinois)

- Lincoln Home National Historic Site (Springfield, Illinois)

- Lincoln Memorial (Washington, D.C.)

- National Museum of American History (Washington, D.C.)

DVDs

There are some great nonfiction DVDs about Abraham Lincoln and the Civil War. As with books, make sure the DVDs you watch for research are nonfiction!

Check your library or video store for these and other nonfiction titles about Lincoln:

- *Abraham Lincoln,* Animated Hero Classics series
  from NEST Complete Learning System

- *Abraham Lincoln,* Great Americans for Children series
  from Schlessinger Media

- *The American Civil War*
  from The History Channel

- *The Assassination of Abraham Lincoln,* American Experience series
  from PBS

The Internet

Many websites have lots of facts about Abraham Lincoln and the Civil War. Some also have games and activities that can help make learning about Lincoln and his era even more fun.

Ask your teacher or your parents to help you find more websites like these:

- abrahamlincoln.org

- alplm.org/timeline/timeline.html

- americancivilwar.com/kids_zone /causes.html

- apples4theteacher.com/holidays /presidents-day/abraham-lincoln

- cr.nps.gov/museum/exhibits/gettex

- enchantedlearning.com/history/us /pres/lincoln

Good luck!

Index

Photographs courtesy of:

Have you read the adventure that matches up with this book?

Don't miss

Magic Tree House® Merlin Mission #19

ABE LINCOLN AT LAST!

Jack and Annie have a new mission to help save Merlin's beloved baby penguin, Penny: they must travel in the magic tree house to meet Abraham Lincoln and get a special feather from him! Can a ragged orphan named Sam help them find Abe? Or will Jack and Annie have to give all their strength and time to helping Sam instead?

Enough cool facts
to fill a tree house!

Jack and Annie have been all over the world in their adventures in the magic tree house. And they've learned lots of incredible facts along the way. Now they want to share them with you! Get ready for a collection of the weirdest, grossest, funniest, most all-around amazing facts that Jack and Annie have ever encountered. It's the ultimate fact attack!

Magic Tree House®

Magic Tree House® Merlin Missions

Magic Tree House®
Super Edition

#1: WORLD AT WAR, 1944

Magic Tree House®
Fact Trackers

DINOSAURS
KNIGHTS AND CASTLES
MUMMIES AND PYRAMIDS
PIRATES
RAIN FORESTS
SPACE
TITANIC
TWISTERS AND OTHER TERRIBLE STORMS
DOLPHINS AND SHARKS
ANCIENT GREECE AND THE OLYMPICS
AMERICAN REVOLUTION
SABERTOOTHS AND THE ICE AGE
PILGRIMS
ANCIENT ROME AND POMPEII
TSUNAMIS AND OTHER NATURAL DISASTERS
POLAR BEARS AND THE ARCTIC
SEA MONSTERS
PENGUINS AND ANTARCTICA
LEONARDO DA VINCI
GHOSTS
LEPRECHAUNS AND IRISH FOLKLORE
RAGS AND RICHES: KIDS IN THE TIME OF
    CHARLES DICKENS
SNAKES AND OTHER REPTILES
DOG HEROES
ABRAHAM LINCOLN

PANDAS AND OTHER ENDANGERED SPECIES
HORSE HEROES
HEROES FOR ALL TIMES
SOCCER
NINJAS AND SAMURAI
CHINA: LAND OF THE EMPEROR'S GREAT
    WALL
SHARKS AND OTHER PREDATORS
VIKINGS
DOGSLEDDING AND EXTREME SPORTS
DRAGONS AND MYTHICAL CREATURES
WORLD WAR II

More Magic Tree House®

GAMES AND PUZZLES FROM THE TREE HOUSE
MAGIC TRICKS FROM THE TREE HOUSE
MY MAGIC TREE HOUSE JOURNAL
MAGIC TREE HOUSE SURVIVAL GUIDE
ANIMAL GAMES AND PUZZLES
MAGIC TREE HOUSE INCREDIBLE FACT BOOK